Raising Career Aspirations of Hispanic Girls

by
Josefina Villamil Tinajero,
Maria Luisa Gonzalez,
and
Florence Dick

Library of Congress Catalog Card Number 91-60199
ISBN 0-87367-320-4
Copyright © 1991 by the Phi Delta Kappa Educational Foundation
Bloomington, Indiana

This fastback is sponsored by the San Antonio Texas Chapter of Phi Delta Kappa, which made a generous contribution toward publication costs.

Table of Contents

Introduction 7

Factors Influencing Educational and Career Aspirations of Hispanic Females 9

History of the Mother-Daughter Program 13

Activities in the Mother-Daughter Program 19
    On-Campus Activities 21
    Off-Campus Activities 28
    The Big Sister Link 30

Program Outcomes 32

References 36

Introduction

Leticia Diaz, a sixth-grader, is one of six children. Her parents speak little English and have only an elementary school education. Both of her older siblings are high school dropouts. Her older sister dropped out of school during her junior year to marry her boyfriend, because, she said, he promised her "the moon and the stars." Her 17-year-old brother works at a nearby grocery store to help the family make ends meet. Her three younger siblings are in elementary school. Although Leticia is an above-average student and excels in math, she has never thought about going to college. In fact, she has never even talked to her friends or her mother about the possibility of attending college.

Rosa Juarez is a 34-year-old single mother with a nine-year-old son and an 11-year-old daughter. Recently divorced, she has just been laid off from her job. She is uncertain about the future. Her morale is low, and she is often depressed. Although she is fluent in English and has a high school diploma, she has never thought about the possibility of going back to school. Mrs. Juarez has a good relationship with her son and daughter but has never talked with them about their plans for the future, their career aspirations, or the possibility of attending college.

Leticia Diaz and and Rosa Juarez are two of approximately 16 million Hispanics residing in the United States. Although a good student, Leticia, like many Hispanics, is statistically at risk of never graduating from high school. Mrs. Juarez, like one-third of the

Hispanics in the U.S., is destined to live in poverty and to be disproportionately represented in low-income occupations.

In this fastback the authors first will examine the conditions, including cultural factors, that put Hispanic females at risk of not completing their education and not aspiring to careers. Then they will describe a program designed to overcome these conditions. It is called the Mother-Daughter Program, a collaborative effort of the University of Texas at El Paso, the YWCA, and three school districts in the El Paso area.

Factors Influencing Educational and Career Aspirations of Hispanic Females

The statistics on educational achievement of Hispanics present a depressing picture. Hispanics, on average, obtain only 7.1 years of schooling — a rate lower than either African-Americans or Anglos — and have a higher dropout rate than either group. In some communities it is estimated that the dropout rate for Hispanics may be as high as 60%. And for Hispanic females the dropout rate is 2% to 3% higher than it is for Hispanic males. They also attend college at a lower rate (Asher 1984; McKay 1988; Hodgkinson 1988).

Hispanic females have been described as the most at-risk of all students. In 1987 less than 8% of adult Hispanic women had completed four or more years of college — the lowest percentage of any major ethnic population in the country and lower than males in any ethnic group (McKay 1988). Furthermore, only 13.7% are employed in managerial and professional occupations (U.S. Department of Commerce 1986, 1987).

Researchers have identified many factors that contribute to the high dropout rate and low educational achievement of Hispanics. According to Johnston and his colleagues (1986), "The pattern of school failure and alienation begins as early as the elementary grades." And dropouts themselves often express disenchantment with school. While they understand the need for an education, school has not been a satisfying experience for them. They perceive the school as an alien environment not capable of understanding them. They do not fit in.

Several studies have found that these negative attitudes are often a result of the school environment. Ekstrom et al. (1986) and Orum (1988) found that the most powerful determinants of school leaving are not family and economic factors, but low grades and disciplinary problems. According to Damico (1989): "Traditional disciplinary sanctions have the effect of convincing potential dropouts that they are not really wanted at school. This communication may be most clear in schools with ethnically diverse student bodies which differ from the faculty and staff who serve them. Schools can, in effect, send out signals to at-risk youth that they are neither able nor worthy to continue to graduation." These signals are powerful influences affecting Hispanic females' feelings of self-esteem and their attitudes toward school.

Andrade (1982) identifies the following conditions as contributing to Hispanic females' negative assessment of the school environment: lack of Hispanic role models (teachers, counselors, administrators), a disproportionate level of referrals to special education classes, low expectations for Hispanics by school personnel, lack of adequate vocational and career counseling for Hispanic women, and stereotypic portrayal of Hispanic women in the curriculum. A female Hispanic student at Stanford University, commenting on the influence of the school setting, says: "Such an educational setting does not provide students with the inspiration or the confidence to achieve. Consequently, a self-fulfilling prophecy is established. Many Hispanics are second-rate students because they get a second-rate education that confines them to the status of second-class citizens" (Zacarias 1990).

Several studies have identified socioeconomic factors associated with the high dropout rate among Hispanics. For example, we know that dropouts tend to come from families of lower socioeconomic status. They come from homes with a weaker educational support system; their parents are less likely to monitor in-school and out-of-school activities; they have fewer study aids in their homes and less opportunity for non-school-related learning activities; and they tend to have mothers with less formal education and lower educational expectations for their offspring.

In the traditionally close-knit Hispanic family, the mother exerts a powerful influence on her children. In a study on the modeling influence of Hispanic mothers, Fleming (1982) found 49% of Hispanic respondents said their mothers influence them a great deal, compared to 40% of Anglo respondents. Thus Hispanic mothers have the potential for influencing their daughters' educational and career choices. However, since most of the mothers are from low socioeconomic backgrounds, they do not model educational and career aspirations for their daughters. Changing this pattern will require early intervention in the education of Hispanic girls.

Commenting on the barriers Hispanic students must overcome, Jaime Escalante (1990), the Los Angeles teacher whose success in teaching advanced mathematics to Hispanic students was the subject of the movie, *Stand and Deliver*, says: "Children of the barrio have enormous obstacles to overcome to get an education. . . . Most of them come from families with incomes below the poverty line. The majority of the parents have not been to college — frequently Mom and Dad have never been to high school — and they may or may not fully appreciate the long-term value of education."

But these barriers can be overcome, says Escalante:

> Minority students may be affected by these barriers, but they are not victims of them. Students can learn to overcome any barrier they will ever face. . . . Some educators maintain the racist ideas that Hispanic students are not as smart as some others and they shy away from courses that require hard work. I have found that to be completely false. When students of any race, ethnicity or economic status are expected to work hard, they will usually rise to the occasion, devote themselves to the task and do the work. If we expect kids to be losers, they will be losers. If we expect them to be winners they will be winners; they rise, or fall, to the level of the expectations of those around them, especially their parents and teachers. If we believe in our children and our students and maintain high expectations and high admiration for

them, they soon will start to believe in themselves. And at that point anything becomes possible. (p. B2)

Given what we know about the socioeconomic and cultural factors impinging on Hispanics, Leticia Diaz has a high probability of following the pattern of her parents and older siblings and becoming a dropout. Rosa Juarez and her two children have a high probablility of becoming a welfare family. However, instead of adding to the statistics, they have become involved in a program designed to encourage Hispanic girls and their mothers to value education, to improve their academic and life skills, and to develop leadership potential, with the goal of completing their education and aspiring to careers. It is called the Mother-Daughter Program.

History of the Mother-Daughter Program

The Mother-Daughter Program began in the fall of 1986 as a pilot project involving the University of Texas at El Paso (UTEP), the YWCA, and three El Paso-area school districts, with the university serving as catalyst. The program was inspired by a similar program conducted by Arizona State University in cooperation with the Phoenix public schools. The program is targeted at high-risk, Hispanic, sixth-grade girls and their mothers from low socioeconomic backgrounds in which no family member has graduated from college.

Currently, the program serves 150 girls and their mothers. Nine schools in three school districts are involved in the program. Principals and teachers in the participating schools select candidates for the program. Participation is voluntary, but the girls must show a potential for academic success based on scores on the Texas Educational Assessment of Minimum Skills (TEAMS) and, more recently, on the Texas Assessment of Academic Skills (TAAS).

The program consists of a series of activities designed to help the girls and their mothers to maintain their interest in school and to raise their educational and career aspirations. The program prepares students for a successful university experience using a team approach that involves mothers directly in the educational process, along with a support network of school coordinators and teachers, YWCA personnel, community leaders, and professionals who serve as role models. Program activities are designed to carry out the following objectives:

- to acquaint the girls and mothers with careers involving higher education,
- to raise the girls' and mothers' aspirations for educational and career opportunities,
- to increase the girls' educational success by improving their academic and life skills,
- to introduce community role models,
- to assist mothers to become more effective role models,
- to provide mothers with skills training and information about community resources, and
- to develop self-esteem and confidence in both mothers and daughters.

Mothers are a central focus of the program, because it is their expectations, their involvement, and their role-modeling that will have a lasting impact on their daughters' educational development (Calderon 1990; Eagle 1989; Fleming 1982; Veres 1974). It is clear from research reviewed earlier that parents of dropouts seldom are involved in their children's school activities. The mothers in the Mother-Daughter Program, however, become intimately involved in their daughters' education. They can see that their daughters' aspirations for higher education are realizable, and so they encourage them to succeed in school. The program teaches mothers how to play a more active role as advisors in their daughters' education.

The program also helps the mothers become better role models for their daughters. Some of the mothers decide to go back to school themselves, in some cases to complete requirements for their high school diplomas, in others to take courses at El Paso Community College or at UTEP. And through the mothers' family and neighborhood networks, the influence of the program extends beyond the girls directly involved.

The program provides the girls with role models and mentors by involving Hispanic female university students and professional women

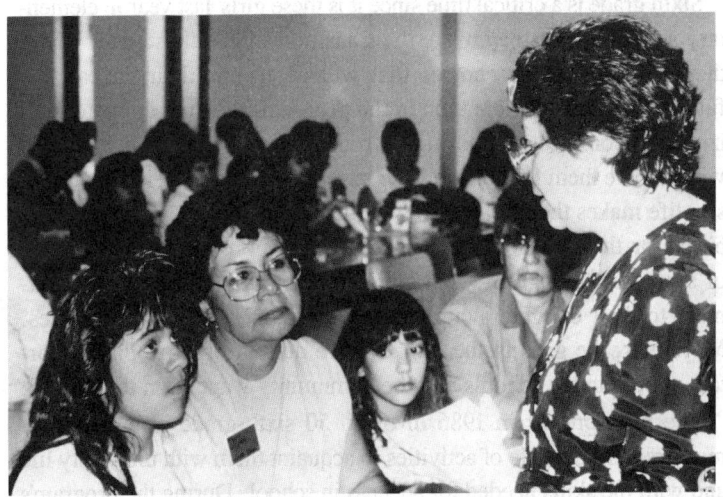

A mother and daughter discuss future options in education and careers with one of the program coordinators.

in the community. Role models and mentors are particularly important for girls whose parents have little formal education and are employed in low-status jobs. UTEP juniors or seniors living in the same neighborhoods as the girls participating in the program volunteer to serve as Big Sisters, and professional Hispanic women in the community serve as important role models.

Although there are many programs that address the dropout problem, the majority are targeted at high school populations. The Mother-Daughter Program, which targets sixth-grade girls, is a deliberate effort to intervene at a time when girls are still open to academic and career options. By the time they reach high school, many Hispanic girls already have made choices that will preclude them from pursuing postsecondary education, thus reducing their chances for success in careers and in life.

Sixth grade is a critical time since it is these girls' last year in elementary school before they make the transition to middle school, where they will be making choices that will determine their educational future. Through participation in the program, the girls come to realize the importance of choosing a strong academic course of study that will prepare them for college. The introduction they receive to university life makes them realize that higher education is a genuine possibility for them if they make informed decisions about their course of study. The program's involvement of mothers fosters a commitment to their daughters' higher education and career opportunities. Moreover, the girls in the program are quick to realize that important people in the schools and the community want them to succeed.

The pilot project in 1986 involved 50 sixth-grade girls and their mothers in a schedule of activities to acquaint them with university life and with the skills needed for success in school. During the program's first year the mothers and daughters toured the UTEP campus, concentrating on the engineering building and the library, and also visited Texas Tech University School of Medicine's Regional Academic Health Center and Thomason General Hospital. Faculty and staff volunteers from the schools and the university and the Big Sisters from UTEP worked with the girls, helping to prepare them for a future as college students. The following spring, the program was expanded to include two school districts; the next year a third school district joined the program, serving a total of 150 girls and their mothers.

From 1986 to 1988, the program operated on an entirely voluntary basis, with in-kind contributions from the university, the school districts, and the YWCA. Administrative support from the participating institutions was critical. During these two years, activities were planned and implemented by committed and dedicated individuals who stretched time and resources to the limit, while continuing to carry their own full workloads.

The key to the Mother-Daughter Program's success is the coalition of institutions working closely together. Representatives from the various institutions serve as members of the Advisory Committee, which oversees the overall direction of the program. The initial Advisory Committee included UTEP's vice president for academic affairs and her assistant, the assistant dean of the College of Education, the YWCA's executive director, and the assistant/associate superintendents from the participating school districts. In addition to the Advisory Committee, a sub-committee, also composed of representatives from the participating institutions, is responsible for the detailed planning of specific activities.

In recent years, grants from several foundations, including substantial funding from the Gannett and Meadows Foundations, have provided some released time for the director, the addition of a full-time program coordinator at UTEP, a part-time coordinator at the YWCA, and part-time secretarial help. This additional staff has provided for a more systematic structuring of the program and for the development of curriculum materials. The curriculum includes packets of materials for developing basic academic skills and for such areas as making decisions, communication, dealing with peer pressure, setting goals, and planning careers. The curriculum packets are available in both English and Spanish, since a majority of the mothers participating in the program speak only Spanish.

The primary costs for implementing the Mother-Daughter Program are for staff salaries, transportation, meals, and refreshments. At first the YWCA and the school districts provided all transportation; more recently, foundation funding has provided bus transportation for all participants. The summer camp on campus is a costly budget item, as is the end-of-year luncheon. Funds from the Gannett and Meadows Foundations, the El Paso Community Foundation, and Southwestern Bell have covered these activities. However, most program activities cost relatively little. Presenters, including members of the American Association of University Women and staff from the university, the YWCA, and school districts, donate their time and talents. Refreshments or sack lunches often are provided free by the participating institutions.

Now in its fifth year, the Mother-Daughter Program is regarded as a model program worthy of replication; and other institutions are assessing the program as a model to implement in their own communities.

With this brief overview of the purpose, organization, and program of the Mother-Daughter Program in El Paso, let us now turn to specific activities in the program in order to see how they affect the lives of Hispanic girls and their mothers.

Activities in the Mother-Daughter Program

The 150 girls and their mothers meet one Saturday each month for a full year, usually in the morning between 8:30 and 12:30. Sessions are held in the local community, in the schools, and at the university. Participants are transported to and from the sessions by school buses. All activities for the mothers and daughters are planned around four important developmental areas: Career Development, Academic Development, Community Life Development, and Personal Development. A series of activity modules for both the mothers and the daughters has been designed for each of these four areas.

For Career Development, for example, the girls participate in a workshop titled, "What Does It Take to Go to College?" and "What Are My Interests and Abilities?" At the same time, the mothers participate in a workshop titled, "What Can My Daughter Be When She Grows Up?" or "What Are My Daughter's Interests and Abilities?" For Academic Development, the girls participate in activities designed to develop their basic academic skills. At the same time, the mothers may attend a session on the topic, "How Can I Assist My Daughter with Her Studies?" Or they may pursue the possibility of enrolling in GED or English classes or attending classes at the community college or the university.

For Community Development, the girls plan and implement a community service project, while the mothers explore community resources that might be used for their own or their daughters' further development. For Personal Development, the girls may discuss family relationships, peer pressure, getting along with others, and feeling better about themselves, while the mothers might participate in a workshop titled, "How Can I Help My Daughter Feel Better About Herself?" or "How Can I Help My Daughter With Her Personal Goals?"

The calendar of activities varies somewhat from year to year. What follows is a sample calendar for one program year:

September — Orientation for all Participants

October — Open House and Tour of University

November — School District Activity and Introduction to Computers

December — Christmas Program and Luncheon

January — Career Day

February — Visit to the Texas Tech School of Medicine

March — Leadership Conference

April — Visit to Junior High Schools, Workshop on Study Skills, Note Taking, and Time Management

May — Awards Luncheon or Cultural Activity

June — Summer Camp on Campus (and Awards Luncheon if not held in May)

July — YWCA Teen Club Activities

August — YWCA Teen Club Activities

The program year begins in September with a general orientation at each of the participating school districts, or all three participating districts may have a joint orientation. The girls and their families are invited, along with the principals from the participating schools, sponsoring teachers, counselors, Big Sisters, and all members of the planning and advisory committees. Program goals and rationale, expectations of participants, and the schedule of activities are explained.

On-Campus Activities

There are four main on-campus activities at UTEP during the school year: Campus Open House and Tour, Career Day, Leadership Conference, and Awards Ceremony/Summer Camp on Campus.

Campus Open House and Tour. This initial event is planned because more than half of the girls have never been to the university. It is designed to familiarize the girls and their mothers with the campus and with university life in general. While there, they learn about the academic preparation required for admission to UTEP and about available scholarships and financial assistance. The girls begin to identify with the university and realize that attending college is a real possibility.

When the buses arrive on campus, they are met by program organizers and a representative from UTEP's Office of Undergraduate Recruitment and Scholarships, who conducts the bus tour of the entire campus. After the tour, the participants register and hear welcoming remarks by university and program officials. Often the director of financial aid will speak on "What It Takes to Go to College," and a representative from the Office of Recruitment and Scholarships will discuss scholarships.

Next, the participants are separated into five or six teams and walk across campus to specific locations for tours and activities. One year, for example, the group was given a tour of the university library, then saw fossil specimens at the Centennial Museum and a robot serving tea at the College of Engineering. Hispanic university students, including members of the Society of Women Engineers, spoke about their interests in engineering, the high school preparation required to major in engineering, the various fields of engineering, and their plans after graduation. The participants then went to the university's writing lab, where the girls performed hands-on activities with computers.

Another year the tour went to the Business Administration building, where the girls and their mothers listened to a panel discussion on "Telling It Like It Is: Women Share Their Moment of Decision." Successful Hispanic university students, serving as role models, shared their personal histories including difficult moments of decision, adversities they faced, and finally the decision-making process they went through that led them on the path to success. Afterward, the mothers attended a workshop on "Money for College, Scholarships, and Financial Aid." Both mothers and daughters then attended a workshop on "Academic Preparation for College." Finally, the girls and their mothers walked to Leech Grove for a picnic before boarding the buses to go home.

This initial experience is important because, for the very first time in their lives, many of the girls begin to think and talk about the real possibility of attending college. The mothers, too, are enthusiastic about the possibility of their daughters' attending college. After one tour, one girl indicated that she was interested in becoming an orthopedic doctor. Because of a birth defect, she wears a prosthesis on her right arm and now wants to help others like herself. Her mother supported her aspirations, commenting that when she heard about the Mother-Daughter Program, she and her daughter joined right away. "I want for her to know what she can study," she said. "She's my hope, the one who tries the hardest in school."

Career Day. An early start in career planning is a key element of the Mother-Daughter Program. Such planning begins when the girls plan their course of study with an eye on the future. Career Day is a special event at the university where the girls and their mothers are introduced to an array of career options. This event brings in panels of Hispanic professional women who share their experiences and are interviewed by the girls and their mothers.

For the past four years, this event has included 25 to 30 professional women — chemists, teachers, doctors, lawyers, interpreters, judges, as well as women in the banking and engineering professions. These professional women serve as role models for the girls and their mothers and make them aware of the advantages of pursuing a college education. They talk about the obstacles they faced while going to college. Many faced language barriers; others had to break away from machismo attitudes in Hispanic families. But most importantly, they tell the girls about career options and about the successes they have had. The girls also become aware of opportunities in nontraditional careers. "Traditionally male jobs offer more money and more opportunities for advancement," one professional woman told the girls. "If you like science and math, go for it!"

After a general presentation, the girls, their mothers, and the professional women meet in small groups to discuss career options available to women. The group sessions provide an opportunity to discuss the academic prerequisites needed in high school to qualify for various career opportunities, including nontraditional fields. While Career Day is designed primarily for the daughters, mothers also benefit from the event. Some mothers decide to go back to school. One mother said, "I thought it was too late for me. But after I listened to all the talk about college and I talked to some professional women who had gone through the same experience of being a single mother with no college education, I said, 'Why not? I can go to college, too!' "

The presentations and small-group sessions with the professional women are usually followed by a joint activity in which the daughters and mothers make "Dream Posters." To make the posters, they cut out pictures from magazines and arrange them on poster board in a way that expresses their ideas and aspirations on "Where Do I See Myself 15 Years from Now?" Mothers and daughters often make separate posters and then share and discuss the ideas expressed in their posters. This activity generates much discussion between the girls and their mothers and is often a very moving experience.

The dream poster activity is one of many opportunities the mothers and daughters have to explore those aspects of their relationship that may be inhibiting the daughters' development. Group leaders also work with the mothers to help them understand what factors might inhibit achievement and whether these factors are societally based or are related to the home environment. The continuing goal is to strengthen the mother-daughter relationship.

Leadership Conference. Another important component of the Mother-Daughter Program is the development of leadership skills. Thus, the third campus event is a leadership conference to which alumnae also are invited, along with a nationally recognized speaker who specializes in leadership and youth. One year the speaker was Dr. Guadalupe Quintanilla, assistant vice president for academic affairs at the University of Houston, who spoke about her hard road to success. After her speech, the girls asked her questions. Another year, in addition to having a nationally recognized speaker, the conference featured a local poet who had written a poem and a story about keeping alive the dream of attending college. His inspirational poem and story dealt with the role of the family, particularly mothers, in encouraging and supporting an education for their daughters. A copy of his poem was presented to all program participants.

The conference begins with a general session followed by small-group sessions conducted by the workshop facilitators. The small-group sessions are designed to help the participants interpret the ideas presented in the general session and then to apply those ideas to the leadership opportunities open to them. By the end of the day, the girls identify a school activity in which they hope to participate and make a positive impact, such as a club, the school newspaper or yearbook, or running for a student-council office.

Another activity to focus the girls' attention on personal and career goals is a booklet developed by the program coordinators titled, "Mujeres de El Paso: Hispanas of Vision." It features profiles of 12 local Hispanic professional women, describing their careers, their education, their recent achievements, and their advice on achieving one's goals. The last two pages of the booklet use the same format as the profiles and provide space for the girls to write their own thoughts about personal and career goals. The format includes the following items:

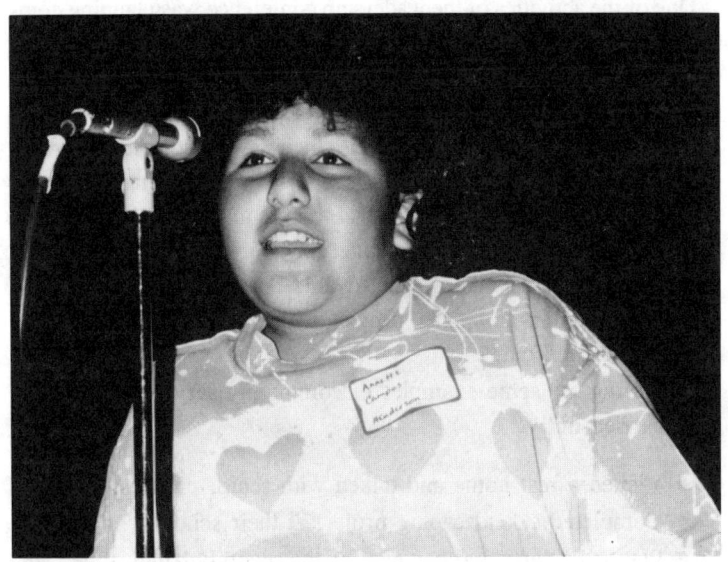

A sixth-grader applies her newly acquired communication skills by asking questions of the keynote speaker at the annual leadership conference.

Occupation: (Write where you would like to work.)

Education: (Write the high school and college you would like to attend.)

Achievements: (Write three things you would like to achieve next year.)

My best leadership experience as a sixth-grade student:

The quality I most admire in the women I've met:

The best advice I've heard on achieving goals:

Three qualities I want to develop as a young woman:

Three goals I've set for myself: (They can be for this year, when you reach high school, or when you grow up.)

One of the activities of the leadership conference was planning community service projects. The girls, together with their Big Sisters, their teachers, and the program coordinator, planned and later implemented a service project in the community or school. This activity not only allowed the girls to exercise their newly acquired leadership skills but, more importantly, it also made them realize that they could contribute to the quality of life in their communities. Each group was required to submit a plan and budget for approval prior to carrying out its project. At the end-of-year Awards Ceremony/Luncheon, each group presented its completed project, using posters to document the activities carried out.

Following are some examples of community service projects the girls carried out:

- Visited a rest home and talked with senior citizens.
- Completed a landscaping project at their school.
- Planned a party and banquet for the severely handicapped students at their school.
- Collected and distributed canned foods at the Central American Refugees Center.
- Collected clothing for a homeless shelter.
- Held an appreciation reception for the fire department.
- Visited the children's ward at the general hospital and distributed baskets of fruit and candy.
- Made instructional materials for the after-school program.

These community projects help to actualize the leadership component of the Mother-Daughter Program and result in lasting benefits to the girls and those they serve.

Awards Ceremony/Summer Camp on Campus. The Awards Ceremony, held in May, honors program graduates with a luncheon and the presentation of certificates by the president of the university and advisory committee members. The girls also receive personal congratulations from their principals and representatives of the various cooperating institutions. The awards luncheon reinforces to the participants that they have accomplished something important by planning for a successful future. The ceremony also recognizes the efforts of others involved in the program: the Big Sisters, principals, sponsoring teachers, planning committee members, advisory committee members, and community volunteers. The awards ceremony also has been combined with a summer camp.

The Summer Camp on Campus is a culminating event of the Mother-Daughter Program. The first camp was held in 1988 on the UTEP campus. Held in June, this event is an intensive two-day immersion into university life when the campus is in full operation. The girls are exposed to dorm life and to college students living in the dorms during the summer session. They attend selected classes with university students and participate in some classroom activities. On the second day, the mothers join their daughters for the awards luncheon.

During the first summer camp, the girls participated in mini-classes in Parasitology, Photography, Spanish Conversation, Creative Arts, Kinesiology, and Teacher Education. They also visited the offices of the *Prospector* (the university's student newspaper), KCOS-TV studio, the Centennial Museum, the Seismic Observatory, the library, the president's office, and the language and science education laboratories. They also completed a set of self-improvement exercises, including Study Skills, Word Processing, Aerobics, and "Finding Your Best Self." In the second year, participants had an opportunity to serve as tutors in a Spanish Conversation class. Recreational activities during the Summer Camp on Campus included a pajama party, story telling, swimming, lunch at the Commons, a pizza party, and a snack in Leech Grove (a popular hangout for UTEP students).

This exposure to university life gives the girls a realistic view of what they can look forward to, and it serves to reaffirm the goals they have been working toward throughout the program year.

Off-Campus Activities

In the months when major events are not scheduled at the university, the girls and their mothers participate in other activities at their schools, the YWCA, or at various sites in the community. Some activities are structured separately for the mothers and daughters, while others are done together. The three school districts use the various curriculum modules developed for the program (study skills, computers, etc.) at the girls' home schools; but sometimes they plan a joint program involving all 150 girls and their mothers. For example, one year the mother-daughter teams from all three school districts met at one site. The girls remained there and worked on computers, participated in a discussion on the perils of drug abuse, and then had time to work on their community projects with their Big Sisters. The mothers, in the meantime, visited the community college campus to learn about various educational opportunities available for adults. Then program personnel worked with the mothers to strengthen their self-esteem as individuals and as members of the Hispanic culture.

Activities also are planned using community resources. Program participants attend the symphony and visit city hall, the historical missions, the public library, and the El Paso Museum of Art. During a visit to the courthouse, mothers and daughters talked with Courtmaster Lupe Rivera-Eggemeyer, who discussed her early interest in law, her education, and her experiences as a lawyer. Participants also have attended city council meetings to learn about local government and about careers in politics. They have talked with County Judge Alicia Chacon and County Commissioner Mary Haynes. These and other community leaders give of their time to share their experiences and to encourage the girls to study and do well in school.

The girls and their mothers also participate in activities sponsored by the YWCA. In cooperation with the university and school districts, the YWCA plans once-a-month summer activities from June through August. These activities have ranged from attending the "Viva El Paso"

A district coordinator for the Mother-Daughter Program meets with some of the sixth-grade girls to discuss their plans for the future.

pageant, to touring the courthouse with a family court judge, to making field observations at the Wilderness Museum.

In the years following the girls' participation in the program, the YWCA, in cooperation with the university, assumes responsibility for organizing the girls into alumnae Y-Teen clubs, with the mothers serving as sponsors and advisors. The girls meet after school or on weekends and participate in a variety of activities. The YWCA also plans workshops for the mothers on such topics as personal health care, dynamics of parenting, drug and alcohol abuse, and money management. All alumnae are invited to the annual leadership conference. Plans are now under way to expand the program so that the girls with their mothers may participate in activities from the sixth grade through their freshman year at college. The El Paso YWCA is working to have its role in the Mother-Daughter Program designated as a National Model to be implemented in YWCAs across the country.

The Big Sister Link

The Big Sisters are a vital component of the Mother-Daughter Program. The Big Sisters are caring Hispanic young women who represent the values that can positively influence the lives of their young charges. As university students, they serve as role models to their "little sisters." Many of them have attended the same elementary schools where the younger girls are currently enrolled.

With help from the UTEP Admissions Office and the school districts, a pool of potential Big Sisters is identified. Often school district coordinators and principals will recommend former graduates now attending UTEP. The women are contacted and extended an invitation to serve as Big Sisters. If they accept, they meet with program coordinators in the early part of the academic year to learn the objectives of the program and to discuss their role in the program. The training covers how to work effectively with groups and techniques for making the weekly calls and house visits and for getting to know the girls and their mothers. Each Big Sister works with approximately 10 girls. The program coordinators try to assign the Big Sisters to girls living in the same neighborhood.

Big Sisters call weekly to establish rapport with the girls and a trusting relationship with the mothers. They encourage their girls to attend program activities, often riding the buses with the girls when they come to activities on campus or in the community. They help their groups plan and execute community projects in their neighborhoods. They also discuss schoolwork, friends, and social life, as well as any personal problems the girls would like to share. Big Sister Rebeca Manriquez, a junior psychology major, reports: "We help out with any problems they might have — with school, family, or anything else that comes up. At first it's hard to set up a line of communication, but then it gets easier. We get a lot of cooperation from the mothers. I feel like I'm part of the family." By the middle of the school year, the girls are best friends with their Big Sisters.

The Big Sister component of the program offers college students the opportunity to provide a valuable service to the Hispanic community. As Magdalena Contreras, a university senior, explains, "I thought it would be interesting and exciting to work with little girls. I welcome the opportunity to talk about my experiences at the university with them."

Program Outcomes

At the time this fastback was being written, the Mother-Daughter Program had enjoyed four years of success in pursuing its ambitious goals of keeping Hispanic girls in school and preparing them for higher education and professional careers. The girls who started in 1986 are now in the 10th grade; they are cheerleaders, student council officers, and members of student organizations. And according to their teachers, they are much more expressive and self-confident. Most important, they have remained in school; attending college is a realistic option for them.

Although it is too early to document how successful the Mother-Daughter Program will be in increasing Hispanic representation in higher education and the professions, program organizers are encouraged by the results so far and believe that the program will have an impact beyond its present scope. Mitchell Ferguson, liaison counselor for one of the participating school districts, describes the effects of the program in this way:

> The Mother-Daughter Program truly makes a difference in the lives and future of our 6th-grade girls and their mothers. I've noticed a positive strengthening of the bond between mother and daughter as they participate together. The UTEP campus tours, evening at the symphony, meeting with community leaders, and activities at the YWCA have raised the self-confidence and leadership skills of the girls. We have

several mothers who are interested in continuing their education or pursuing a career they once felt was out of their reach. The mothers have become effective role models for their daughters and are helping them prepare for success.

Ferguson goes on to say that everyone who participates benefits. "The teachers and the Big Sisters truly care about nurturing the girls and in turn get caring back from them."

Christine Rios, coordinating teacher at one of the participating schools, reports: "The Mother-Daughter Program has given many of the girls a wonderful opportunity to see a broader view of what the world has to offer Hispanic women . . . to see successful examples of women who are able to have a career and a family."

One mother said of the program, "We had very beautiful experiences. My daughter has improved a lot in her studies; she tries to be better. It is a very beautiful program that helps us to advance ourselves a lot."

Big Sister Manriquez summed it up best: "I know in the future these girls will make it."

Before they enter the program, the girls are uncertain about their future. After their year in the program, they know the direction their education is taking them, they talk about careers and college, and they are closer to their mothers. Mothers comment that they have higher expectations for their daughters and for their other children, and they now take a more active role in their daughters' education. They now talk of their daughters attending college as a reality. It's no longer "if my daughter goes to college," it's "when my daughter goes to college."

So far, the girls have indicated, through personal interviews and questionnaires, that they have learned a lot about different academic fields. Campus visits and classroom exercises have provided them with a flavor of university life, a better understanding of the expectations for college students, and the preparation necessary to succeed. They also report that they have learned about the importance of staying in school, the value of education, and the importance of studying and earning good grades. They now believe they have confidence to accomplish anything they want to do.

The mothers report that they now realize the importance of their involvement and support of their children's education, and they are more positive about the possibility of their daughters attending college. Participation in the program has made them realize that higher education is a genuine possibility for their daughters and that their daughters can enhance their opportunities by studying and by making informed decisions concerning courses of study.

Leticia Diaz, whom you met at the beginning of this fastback, was in the first group of girls who participated in the Mother-Daughter Program. She is now a freshman in high school and already knows she wants to be a banker. An honor student in high school and active in extracurricular activities, Leticia often talks about her dreams of becoming a banker. At home, she likes to pretend she's a banker and has her own make-believe bank office complete with bank statements, play money, and fictional customers. Leticia's mother constantly encourages her to think about going to college. "I would love it because I think education is the basis of success in life," she says.

Rosa Juarez, whom you met earlier, also went through the first Mother-Daughter Program with her daughter, Jessica. The program's seminars and tours proved to be as helpful to Mrs. Juarez as to her daughter. Although the program's primary purpose was to encourage girls like Jessica to stay in school and prepare for college, today it is Rosa Juarez who carries a student ID card from the University of Texas at El Paso. She is currently a junior working toward her bachelor's degree in education. Her daughter, Jessica, and her son, who was having problems when she first joined the program, are honors students, and both plan to follow their mother's path to college.

Recently she said, "Our Hispanic little girls are in trouble. We desperately needed a program like this. This program has shown them that Hispanic women can make it in the world." She maintains that her experience is no isolated success story but rather is a testament to how struggling single mothers can achieve once someone shows them the possibilities. She has now started her own grassroots education effort, urging other women in her housing project to head back to school. Food stamps and subsidized housing may still support her family, but Rosa Juarez refuses to view these as marks of continuing poverty. They are temporary help, she said, to be paid back once she starts her teaching career.

And so the efforts of the University of Texas and its collaborators continue. A new group of 150 Hispanic girls and their mothers are now involved in the program. Participants from previous years continue as alumnae. In years to come, perhaps they will serve as Big Sisters or facilitators for other young girls. Despite the length of time required to see the outcome, the Mother-Daughter Program appears to be on target. It builds on family support, particularly the bonding between mother and daughter, and can lead to a better preparation and higher aspirations of young Hispanic women for college and careers.

References

Andrade, Sally J. *Young Hispanics in the United States — Their Aspirations for the Future: Findings from Two National Surveys.* Austin, Texas: Center for Applied Systems Analysis, 1982.

Asher, C. *Helping Hispanic Students to Complete High School and Enter College.* New York: Teachers College, Columbia University, ERIC Clearinghouse on Urban Education, 1984.

Calderon, Margarita. *Literacy Patterns of Hispanic Head Start Parents.* El Paso: Family Literacy Project, Head Start Program, 1990.

Damico, Sandra Bowen. "Staying in School: Social Learning Factors Which Lead to Retention." Paper presented at the annual meeting of the American Educational Research Association, San Francisco, 1989.

Eagle, Eva. "Socioeconomic Status, Family Structure, and Parental Involvement: The Correlates of Achievement." Paper presented at the annual meeting of the American Educational Research Association, San Francisco, 1989.

Ekstrom, Ruth B.; Goertz, Margaret E.; Pollack, Judith M.; and Rock, Donald A. "Who Drops Out and Why: Findings from a National Study." *Teachers College Record* 87 (Spring 1986): 356-73.

Escalante, Jaime. "All Children Can Learn to Succeed — When They Have Ganas." *El Paso Times*, 27 August 1990, p. B2.

Fleming, Lizanne. *Parental Influence on the Educational and Career Decision of Hispanic Youth.* Washington, D.C.: National Council of La Raza, 1982.

Hodgkinson, Harold L. "People and Populations: The Shape of Our Future." Presentation at the University of Texas at El Paso Tomas Rivera Conference Center, September 1988.

Intercultural Development Research Association (IDRA). *Texas School Dropout Survey Project: A Summary of Findings*. San Antonio, 1986.

Johnston, J. Howard; Markle, Glenn C.; and Harshbarger, Margaret. "What Research Says — About Dropouts." *Middle School Journal* 17 (August 1986): 8-11.

McKay, Emily Gantz. *Changing Hispanic Demographics*. Washington, D.C.: National Council of La Raza, 1988.

Orum, Lori S. *Making Education Work for Hispanic Americans: Some Promising Community-Based Practices*. Los Angeles: National Council of La Raza, Los Angeles Program Office, 1988.

Paulu, Nancy., ed. *Dealing with Dropouts: The Urban Superintendents' Call to Action*. Washington, D.C.: U.S. Government Printing Office, 1987.

Rodriguez, Justin F. "Youth Employment: A Needs Assessment." *The Vice President's Task Force on Youth Employment: A Review of Youth Employment Problems, Programs and Policies*. vol. 1. Washington, D.C.: U.S. Government Printing Office, 1980.

Taggart, Robert. "The Youth Employment Program: A Sequential and Developmental Perspective." *The Vice President's Task Force on Youth Employment: A Review of Youth Employment Problems, Programs and Policies*. vol. 1. Washington, D.C.: U.S. Government Printing Office, 1980.

U.S. Department of Commerce. Bureau of Census, 1986, 1987.

U.S. Department of Labor, Women's Bureau. "Women of Hispanic Origin in the United States Labor Force." In *Facts on U.S. Working Women*. Fact Sheet No. 88-3. September 1988.

Veres, Helen C. "Career Choice and Career Commitment of Two-Year College Women." Paper presented at the annual meeting of the American Educational Research Association, Chicago, 1974.

Zacarias, Karen. "Now That I've Made It into Mainstream I Must Not Be Hispanic." *El Paso Times*, 28 August 1990, p. B4.